## THIS LEDGER AND ALL RECIPES HEREIN
## ARE THE SOLE PROPERTY OF:

BREWERS' LEDGER
COPYRIGHT © 2014 ANTONY PAWELA | ALL RIGHTS RESERVED
ISBN-13: 978-1514351819 | ISBN-10: 1514351811
BREWERSLEDGER.COM | BREWERSLEDGER@GMAIL.COM

# TABLE OF CONTENTS

# BREW ONE

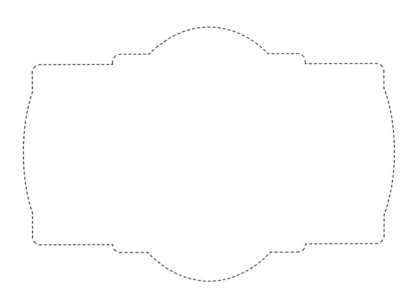

STYLE

BREWED                          FINISHED

OG                              FG

ABV                             IBU

VOLUME                          EFFICIENCY

$Ca^{+2}$      $Mg^{+2}$      $Na^+$      $Cl^-$      $So_4^{-2}$      Alk      pH

# 🌾 GRAIN

| | % | WEIGHT | GU |
|---|---|---|---|
| | | | |
| | | | |
| | | | |
| | | | |
| | | | |
| | | | |
| | | | |

# 💧 WATER

| | | | |
|---|---|---|---|
| | | | |
| | | | |

# 🕐 MASH

| | VOLUME | STRIKE° | REST° | TIME | GRAVITY |
|---|---|---|---|---|---|
| | | | | | |
| | | | | | |
| | | | | | |
| | | | | | |
| | | | | | |

## 🌰 HOPS

| | OZ | AA% | IBU | MIN |
|---|---|---|---|---|
| | | | | |
| | | | | |
| | | | | |
| | | | | |
| | | | | |
| | | | | |
| | | | | |
| | | | | |

## 🧪 YEAST

| | AMOUNT | PITCH° |
|---|---|---|
| | | |

## 🕐 FERMENT

| | DATE | TEMP° | GRAVITY |
|---|---|---|---|
| | | | |
| | | | |
| | | | |
| | | | |
| | | | |

# 1 🍾 PACKAGE

| VOLUME | TEMP | CO2 | PRIME |
|--------|------|-----|-------|
|        |      |     |       |

# 🍺 NOTES

AROMA

APPEARANCE

FLAVOR

MOUTHFEEL

OVERALL

# BREW TWO

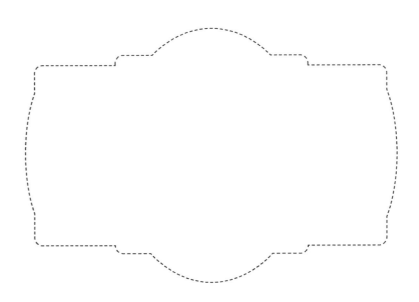

STYLE

BREWED                          FINISHED

OG                              FG

ABV                             IBU

VOLUME                          EFFICIENCY

Ca⁺²     Mg⁺²     Na⁺     Cl⁻     So₄⁻²     Alk     pH

## 🌾 GRAIN

| | % | WEIGHT | GU |
|---|---|---|---|
| | | | |
| | | | |
| | | | |
| | | | |
| | | | |
| | | | |
| | | | |

## 💧 WATER

| | | | |
|---|---|---|---|
| | | | |
| | | | |

## 🕐 MASH

| VOLUME | STRIKE° | REST° | TIME | GRAVITY |
|---|---|---|---|---|
| | | | | |
| | | | | |
| | | | | |
| | | | | |
| | | | | |

# 🌿 HOPS

| | OZ | AA% | IBU | MIN |
|---|---|---|---|---|
| | | | | |
| | | | | |
| | | | | |
| | | | | |
| | | | | |
| | | | | |
| | | | | |

# 🧪 YEAST

| | AMOUNT | PITCH° |
|---|---|---|
| | | |

# 🕐 FERMENT

| | DATE | TEMP° | GRAVITY |
|---|---|---|---|
| | | | |
| | | | |
| | | | |
| | | | |

# 🍾 PACKAGE

| VOLUME | TEMP | CO2 | PRIME |
|--------|------|-----|-------|
|        |      |     |       |

# 🍺 NOTES

AROMA

APPEARANCE

FLAVOR

MOUTHFEEL

OVERALL

# BREW THREE

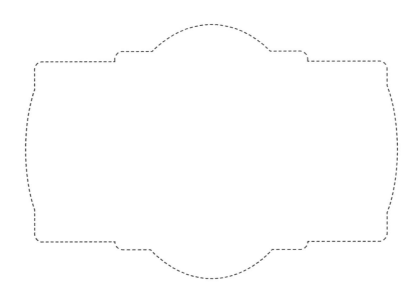

STYLE

BREWED                                  FINISHED

OG                                      FG

ABV                                     IBU

VOLUME                                  EFFICIENCY

| $Ca^{+2}$ | $Mg^{+2}$ | $Na^+$ | $Cl^-$ | $So_4^{-2}$ | Alk | pH |
|---|---|---|---|---|---|---|

## 🌾 GRAIN

| | % | WEIGHT | GU |
|---|---|---|---|
| | | | |
| | | | |
| | | | |
| | | | |
| | | | |
| | | | |
| | | | |

## 💧 WATER

| | | | | |
|---|---|---|---|---|
| | | | | |
| | | | | |
| | | | | |

## 🕐 MASH

| | VOLUME | STRIKE° | REST° | TIME | GRAVITY |
|---|---|---|---|---|---|
| | | | | | |
| | | | | | |
| | | | | | |
| | | | | | |
| | | | | | |

# 🌰 HOPS

| OZ | AA% | IBU | MIN |
|----|-----|-----|-----|
|    |     |     |     |
|    |     |     |     |
|    |     |     |     |
|    |     |     |     |
|    |     |     |     |
|    |     |     |     |
|    |     |     |     |

# 🧪 YEAST

| AMOUNT | PITCH° |
|--------|--------|
|        |        |
|        |        |

# 🕐 FERMENT

| DATE | TEMP° | GRAVITY |
|------|-------|---------|
|      |       |         |
|      |       |         |
|      |       |         |
|      |       |         |

# 🍾 PACKAGE

| VOLUME | TEMP | CO2 | PRIME |
|--------|------|-----|-------|
|        |      |     |       |

3

# 🍺 NOTES

AROMA

APPEARANCE

FLAVOR

MOUTHFEEL

OVERALL

# BREW FOUR

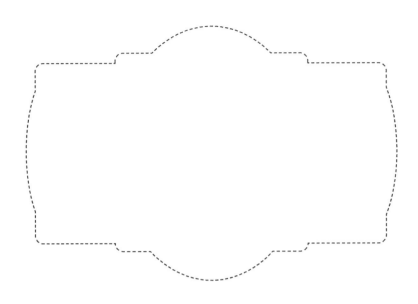

STYLE

BREWED                          FINISHED

OG                              FG

ABV                             IBU

VOLUME                          EFFICIENCY

| $Ca^{+2}$ | $Mg^{+2}$ | $Na^+$ | $Cl^-$ | $So_4^{-2}$ | Alk | pH |
|---|---|---|---|---|---|---|

# 🌾 GRAIN

| % | WEIGHT | GU |
|---|--------|-----|
|   |        |     |
|   |        |     |
|   |        |     |
|   |        |     |
|   |        |     |
|   |        |     |
|   |        |     |
|   |        |     |

4

# 💧 WATER

|   |   |   |   |
|---|---|---|---|
|   |   |   |   |
|   |   |   |   |
|   |   |   |   |

# 🕐 MASH

| VOLUME | STRIKE° | REST° | TIME | GRAVITY |
|--------|---------|-------|------|---------|
|        |         |       |      |         |
|        |         |       |      |         |
|        |         |       |      |         |
|        |         |       |      |         |
|        |         |       |      |         |

# 🌿 HOPS

| | OZ | AA% | IBU | MIN |
|---|---|---|---|---|
| | | | | |
| | | | | |
| | | | | |
| | | | | |
| | | | | |
| | | | | |
| | | | | |
| | | | | |

# ⚗️ YEAST

| | AMOUNT | PITCH° |
|---|---|---|
| | | |

# 🕐 FERMENT

| | DATE | TEMP° | GRAVITY |
|---|---|---|---|
| | | | |
| | | | |
| | | | |
| | | | |

#  PACKAGE

| VOLUME | TEMP | CO2 | PRIME |
|--------|------|-----|-------|
|        |      |     |       |

4

# NOTES

AROMA

APPEARANCE

FLAVOR

MOUTHFEEL

OVERALL

# BREW FIVE

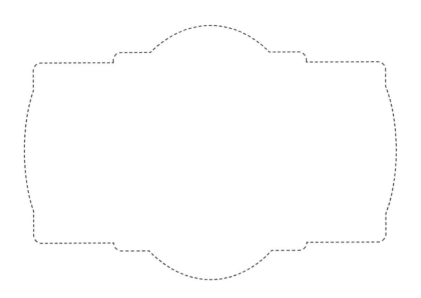

STYLE

BREWED                                    FINISHED

OG                                        FG

ABV                                       IBU

VOLUME                                    EFFICIENCY

Ca$^{+2}$          Mg$^{+2}$        Na$^+$        Cl$^-$         So$_4$$^{-2}$        Alk        pH

# 🌾 GRAIN

| | % | WEIGHT | GU |
|---|---|---|---|
| | | | |
| | | | |
| | | | |
| | | | |
| | | | |
| | | | |
| | | | |

# 💧 WATER

| | | | | |
|---|---|---|---|---|
| | | | | |
| | | | | |
| | | | | |

# 🕐 MASH

| VOLUME | STRIKE° | REST° | TIME | GRAVITY |
|---|---|---|---|---|
| | | | | |
| | | | | |
| | | | | |
| | | | | |
| | | | | |

# 🌿 HOPS

| | OZ | AA% | IBU | MIN |
|---|---|---|---|---|
| | | | | |
| | | | | |
| | | | | |
| | | | | |
| | | | | |
| | | | | |
| | | | | |

# ⚗ YEAST

| | AMOUNT | PITCH° |
|---|---|---|
| | | |
| | | |

# 🕐 FERMENT

| | DATE | TEMP° | GRAVITY |
|---|---|---|---|
| | | | |
| | | | |
| | | | |
| | | | |
| | | | |

5

#  PACKAGE

| VOLUME | TEMP | CO2 | PRIME |
|--------|------|-----|-------|
|        |      |     |       |

# 🍺 NOTES

AROMA

APPEARANCE

FLAVOR

MOUTHFEEL

OVERALL

# BREW SIX

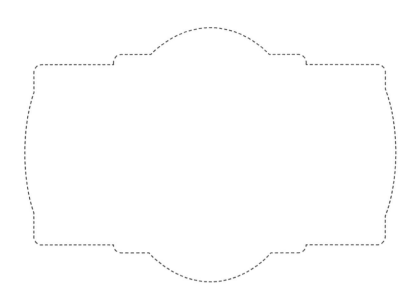

STYLE

| | |
|---|---|
| BREWED | FINISHED |
| OG | FG |
| ABV | IBU |
| VOLUME | EFFICIENCY |

| $Ca^{+2}$ | $Mg^{+2}$ | $Na^+$ | $Cl^-$ | $So_4^{-2}$ | Alk | pH |
|---|---|---|---|---|---|---|

## 🌾 GRAIN

| | % | WEIGHT | GU |
|---|---|---|---|
| | | | |
| | | | |
| | | | |
| | | | |
| | | | |
| | | | |
| | | | |

## 💧 WATER

| | | | | |
|---|---|---|---|---|
| | | | | |
| | | | | |
| | | | | |

## 🕐 MASH

| VOLUME | STRIKE° | REST° | TIME | GRAVITY |
|---|---|---|---|---|
| | | | | |
| | | | | |
| | | | | |
| | | | | |
| | | | | |
| | | | | |

# 🍺 HOPS

| | OZ | AA% | IBU | MIN |
|---|---|---|---|---|
| | | | | |
| | | | | |
| | | | | |
| | | | | |
| | | | | |
| | | | | |

# ⚗ YEAST

| | AMOUNT | PITCH° |
|---|---|---|
| | | |
| | | |

# 🕐 FERMENT

| | DATE | TEMP° | GRAVITY |
|---|---|---|---|
| | | | |
| | | | |
| | | | |
| | | | |

# 🍾 PACKAGE

| VOLUME | TEMP | CO2 | PRIME |
|--------|------|-----|-------|
|        |      |     |       |

# 🍺 NOTES

6

AROMA

APPEARANCE

FLAVOR

MOUTHFEEL

OVERALL

# BREW SEVEN

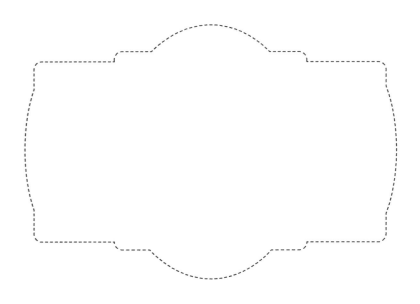

STYLE

BREWED                          FINISHED

OG                             FG

ABV                            IBU

VOLUME                         EFFICIENCY

$Ca^{+2}$      $Mg^{+2}$      $Na^+$      $Cl^-$      $So_4^{-2}$      Alk      pH

29

# 🌾 GRAIN

| | % | WEIGHT | GU |
|---|---|---|---|
| | | | |
| | | | |
| | | | |
| | | | |
| | | | |
| | | | |
| | | | |

# 💧 WATER

| | | | | |
|---|---|---|---|---|
| | | | | |
| | | | | |
| | | | | |

# 🕐 MASH

| VOLUME | STRIKE° | REST° | TIME | GRAVITY |
|---|---|---|---|---|
| | | | | |
| | | | | |
| | | | | |
| | | | | |
| | | | | |

# 🌺 HOPS

| | OZ | AA% | IBU | MIN |
|---|---|---|---|---|
| | | | | |
| | | | | |
| | | | | |
| | | | | |
| | | | | |
| | | | | |
| | | | | |

7

# ⚗️ YEAST

| | AMOUNT | PITCH° |
|---|---|---|
| | | |
| | | |

# 🕐 FERMENT

| | DATE | TEMP° | GRAVITY |
|---|---|---|---|
| | | | |
| | | | |
| | | | |
| | | | |

# 🍾 PACKAGE

| VOLUME | TEMP | CO2 | PRIME |
|--------|------|-----|-------|
|        |      |     |       |

# 🍺 NOTES

AROMA

APPEARANCE

FLAVOR

MOUTHFEEL

OVERALL

# BREW EIGHT

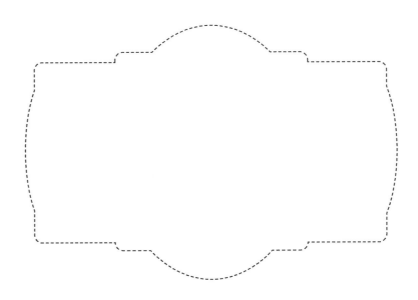

8

STYLE

BREWED

FINISHED

OG

FG

ABV

IBU

VOLUME

EFFICIENCY

| Ca$^{+2}$ | Mg$^{+2}$ | Na$^{+}$ | Cl$^{-}$ | So$_4^{-2}$ | Alk | pH |
|---|---|---|---|---|---|---|

## 🌾 GRAIN

| | % | WEIGHT | GU |
|---|---|---|---|
| | | | |
| | | | |
| | | | |
| | | | |
| | | | |
| | | | |
| | | | |
| | | | |

8

## 💧 WATER

| | | | | |
|---|---|---|---|---|
| | | | | |
| | | | | |
| | | | | |

## 🕐 MASH

| | VOLUME | STRIKE° | REST° | TIME | GRAVITY |
|---|---|---|---|---|---|
| | | | | | |
| | | | | | |
| | | | | | |
| | | | | | |
| | | | | | |

## 🍺 HOPS

| | OZ | AA% | IBU | MIN |
|---|---|---|---|---|
| | | | | |
| | | | | |
| | | | | |
| | | | | |
| | | | | |
| | | | | |
| | | | | |
| | | | | |

8

## ⚗️ YEAST

| | AMOUNT | PITCH° |
|---|---|---|
| | | |
| | | |

## 🕐 FERMENT

| | DATE | TEMP° | GRAVITY |
|---|---|---|---|
| | | | |
| | | | |
| | | | |
| | | | |
| | | | |

# 🍾 PACKAGE

| VOLUME | TEMP | CO2 | PRIME |
|--------|------|-----|-------|
|        |      |     |       |

# 🍺 NOTES

AROMA

APPEARANCE

FLAVOR

MOUTHFEEL

OVERALL

# BREW NINE

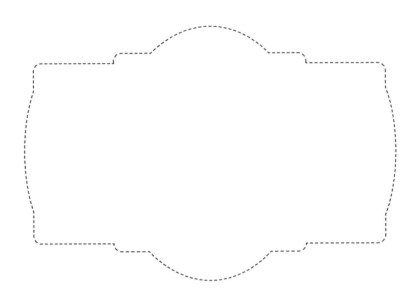

STYLE

BREWED                          FINISHED

OG                              FG

ABV                             IBU

VOLUME                          EFFICIENCY

| $Ca^{+2}$ | $Mg^{+2}$ | $Na^+$ | $Cl^-$ | $So_4^{-2}$ | Alk | pH |
|-----------|-----------|--------|--------|-------------|-----|-----|
|           |           |        |        |             |     |     |

# 🌾 GRAIN

|  | % | WEIGHT | GU |
|---|---|---|---|
|  |  |  |  |
|  |  |  |  |
|  |  |  |  |
|  |  |  |  |
|  |  |  |  |
|  |  |  |  |
|  |  |  |  |

# 💧 WATER

|  |  |  |  |  |
|---|---|---|---|---|
|  |  |  |  |  |
|  |  |  |  |  |
|  |  |  |  |  |

# 🕐 MASH

| VOLUME | STRIKE° | REST° | TIME | GRAVITY |
|---|---|---|---|---|
|  |  |  |  |  |
|  |  |  |  |  |
|  |  |  |  |  |
|  |  |  |  |  |
|  |  |  |  |  |

# 🌿 HOPS

| | OZ | AA% | IBU | MIN |
|---|---|---|---|---|
| | | | | |
| | | | | |
| | | | | |
| | | | | |
| | | | | |
| | | | | |

9

# 🧪 YEAST

| | AMOUNT | PITCH° |
|---|---|---|
| | | |
| | | |

# 🕐 FERMENT

| | DATE | TEMP° | GRAVITY |
|---|---|---|---|
| | | | |
| | | | |
| | | | |
| | | | |

# 🍾 PACKAGE

| VOLUME | TEMP | CO2 | PRIME |
|--------|------|-----|-------|
|        |      |     |       |

# 🍺 NOTES

AROMA

APPEARANCE

FLAVOR

MOUTHFEEL

OVERALL

# BREW TEN

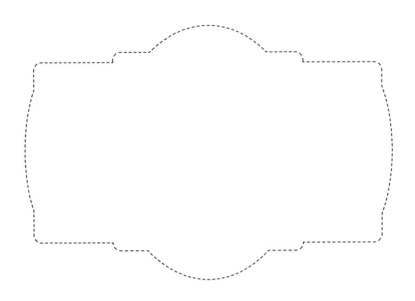

STYLE

BREWED                          FINISHED

OG                              FG

ABV                             IBU

VOLUME                          EFFICIENCY

$Ca^{+2}$      $Mg^{+2}$      $Na^+$      $Cl^-$      $So_4^{-2}$      Alk      pH

## 🌾 GRAIN

| | % | WEIGHT | GU |
|---|---|---|---|
| | | | |
| | | | |
| | | | |
| | | | |
| | | | |
| | | | |
| | | | |
| | | | |
| | | | |

## 💧 WATER

| | | | | |
|---|---|---|---|---|
| | | | | |
| | | | | |
| | | | | |

## 🕐 MASH

| VOLUME | STRIKE° | REST° | TIME | GRAVITY |
|---|---|---|---|---|
| | | | | |
| | | | | |
| | | | | |
| | | | | |
| | | | | |
| | | | | |

## 🍺 HOPS

| | OZ | AA% | IBU | MIN |
|---|---|---|---|---|
| | | | | |
| | | | | |
| | | | | |
| | | | | |
| | | | | |
| | | | | |
| | | | | |

## ⚗ YEAST

| | AMOUNT | PITCH° |
|---|---|---|
| | | |
| | | |

## 🕐 FERMENT

| | DATE | TEMP° | GRAVITY |
|---|---|---|---|
| | | | |
| | | | |
| | | | |
| | | | |
| | | | |

# 🍾 PACKAGE

| | VOLUME | TEMP | CO2 | PRIME |
|---|---|---|---|---|
| | | | | |

# 🍺 NOTES

AROMA

APPEARANCE

FLAVOR

MOUTHFEEL

OVERALL

# BREW ELEVEN

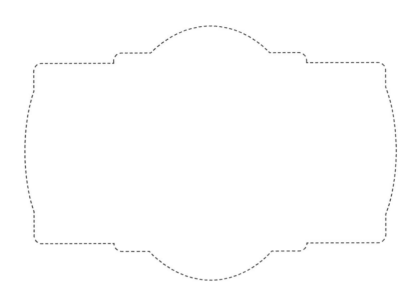

STYLE

| BREWED | | | | FINISHED | | |
|---|---|---|---|---|---|---|
| OG | | | | FG | | |
| ABV | | | | IBU | | |
| VOLUME | | | | EFFICIENCY | | |

| $Ca^{+2}$ | $Mg^{+2}$ | $Na^+$ | $Cl^-$ | $So_4^{-2}$ | Alk | pH |
|---|---|---|---|---|---|---|

# 🌾 GRAIN

| | % | WEIGHT | GU |
|---|---|---|---|
| | | | |
| | | | |
| | | | |
| | | | |
| | | | |
| | | | |
| | | | |
| | | | |

# 💧 WATER

| | | | |
|---|---|---|---|
| | | | |
| | | | |
| | | | |

# 🕐 MASH

| VOLUME | STRIKE° | REST° | TIME | GRAVITY |
|---|---|---|---|---|
| | | | | |
| | | | | |
| | | | | |
| | | | | |
| | | | | |
| | | | | |

# 🌺 HOPS

| | OZ | AA% | IBU | MIN |
|---|---|---|---|---|
| | | | | |
| | | | | |
| | | | | |
| | | | | |
| | | | | |
| | | | | |
| | | | | |

# ⚗ YEAST

| | AMOUNT | PITCH° |
|---|---|---|
| | | |

# 🕐 FERMENT

| | DATE | TEMP° | GRAVITY |
|---|---|---|---|
| | | | |
| | | | |
| | | | |
| | | | |

# 🍾 PACKAGE

| VOLUME | TEMP | CO2 | PRIME |
|--------|------|-----|-------|
|        |      |     |       |

# 🍺 NOTES

AROMA

APPEARANCE

FLAVOR

MOUTHFEEL

OVERALL

# BREW TWELVE

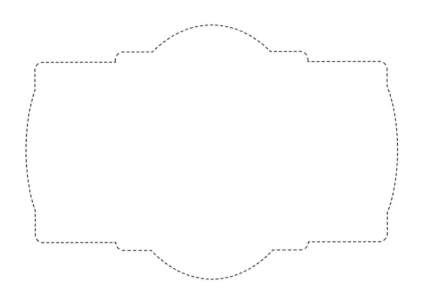

12

STYLE

BREWED                                      FINISHED

OG                                          FG

ABV                                         IBU

VOLUME                                      EFFICIENCY

| $Ca^{+2}$ | $Mg^{+2}$ | $Na^+$ | $Cl^-$ | $So_4^{-2}$ | Alk | pH |
|-----------|-----------|--------|--------|-------------|-----|-----|
|           |           |        |        |             |     |     |

# 🌾 GRAIN

| | % | WEIGHT | GU |
|---|---|---|---|
| | | | |
| | | | |
| | | | |
| | | | |
| | | | |
| | | | |
| | | | |

# 💧 WATER

| | | | |
|---|---|---|---|
| | | | |
| | | | |

# 🕐 MASH

| | VOLUME | STRIKE° | REST° | TIME | GRAVITY |
|---|---|---|---|---|---|
| | | | | | |
| | | | | | |
| | | | | | |
| | | | | | |
| | | | | | |
| | | | | | |

# 🍺 HOPS

| | OZ | AA% | IBU | MIN |
|---|---|---|---|---|
| | | | | |
| | | | | |
| | | | | |
| | | | | |
| | | | | |
| | | | | |
| | | | | |

# ⚗️ YEAST

| | AMOUNT | PITCH° |
|---|---|---|
| | | |

# 🕐 FERMENT

| | TIME | TEMP° | GRAVITY |
|---|---|---|---|
| | | | |
| | | | |
| | | | |
| | | | |

# 🍾 PACKAGE

| VOLUME | TEMP | CO2 | PRIME |
|--------|------|-----|-------|
|        |      |     |       |

# 🍺 NOTES

AROMA

APPEARANCE

12

FLAVOR

MOUTHFEEL

OVERALL

# BREW THIRTEEN

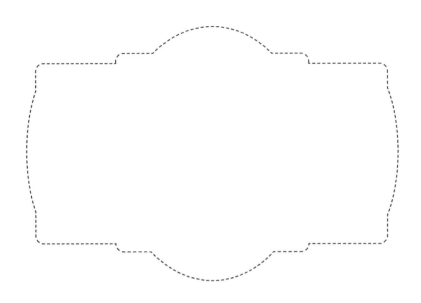

STYLE

BREWED                          FINISHED

OG                              FG

ABV                             IBU

VOLUME                          EFFICIENCY

| $Ca^{+2}$ | $Mg^{+2}$ | $Na^+$ | $Cl^-$ | $So_4^{-2}$ | Alk | pH |
|------|------|------|------|------|------|------|

## 🌾 GRAIN

| | % | WEIGHT | GU |
|---|---|---|---|
| | | | |
| | | | |
| | | | |
| | | | |
| | | | |
| | | | |
| | | | |

## 💧 WATER

| | | | | |
|---|---|---|---|---|
| | | | | |
| | | | | |
| | | | | |

## 🕐 MASH

| | VOLUME | STRIKE° | REST° | TIME | GRAVITY |
|---|---|---|---|---|---|
| | | | | | |
| | | | | | |
| | | | | | |
| | | | | | |
| | | | | | |
| | | | | | |

## 🍺 HOPS

| | OZ | AA% | IBU | MIN |
|---|---|---|---|---|
| | | | | |
| | | | | |
| | | | | |
| | | | | |
| | | | | |
| | | | | |
| | | | | |

## ⚗️ YEAST

| | AMOUNT | PITCH° |
|---|---|---|
| | | |

## 🕐 FERMENT

| | TIME | TEMP° | GRAVITY |
|---|---|---|---|
| | | | |
| | | | |
| | | | |
| | | | |

# 🍾 PACKAGE

| VOLUME | TEMP | CO2 | PRIME |
|--------|------|-----|-------|
|        |      |     |       |

# 🍺 NOTES

AROMA

APPEARANCE

FLAVOR

MOUTHFEEL

OVERALL

13

# BREW FOURTEEN

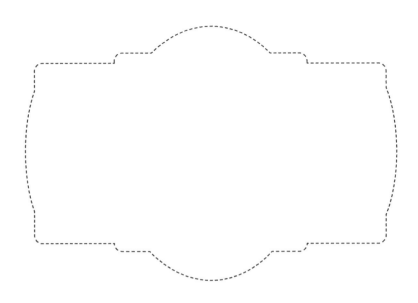

STYLE

BREWED                                    FINISHED

OG                                        FG

ABV                                       IBU

VOLUME                                    EFFICIENCY

| $Ca^{+2}$ | $Mg^{+2}$ | $Na^+$ | $Cl^-$ | $So_4^{-2}$ | Alk | pH |
|------|------|------|------|------|------|------|

# 🌾 GRAIN

| | % | WEIGHT | GU |
|---|---|---|---|
| | | | |
| | | | |
| | | | |
| | | | |
| | | | |
| | | | |
| | | | |

# 💧 WATER

| | | | |
|---|---|---|---|
| | | | |
| | | | |
| | | | |

# 🕐 MASH

| VOLUME | STRIKE° | REST° | TIME | GRAVITY |
|---|---|---|---|---|
| | | | | |
| | | | | |
| | | | | |
| | | | | |
| | | | | |
| | | | | |

14

# 🌿 HOPS

| | OZ | AA% | IBU | MIN |
|---|---|---|---|---|
| | | | | |
| | | | | |
| | | | | |
| | | | | |
| | | | | |
| | | | | |

# 🧪 YEAST

| | AMOUNT | PITCH° |
|---|---|---|
| | | |
| | | |

14

# 🕐 FERMENT

| | TIME | TEMP° | GRAVITY |
|---|---|---|---|
| | | | |
| | | | |
| | | | |
| | | | |

# 🍾 PACKAGE

| VOLUME | TEMP | CO2 | PRIME |
|--------|------|-----|-------|
|        |      |     |       |

# 🍺 NOTES

AROMA

APPEARANCE

FLAVOR

14

MOUTHFEEL

OVERALL

# BREW FIFTEEN

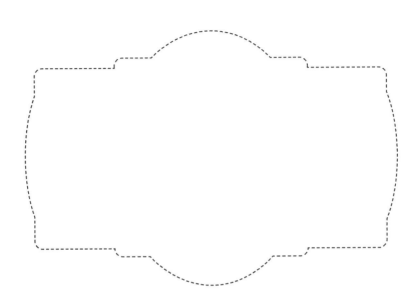

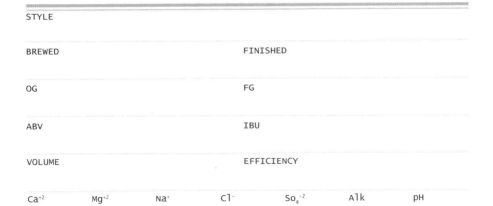

STYLE

BREWED                          FINISHED

OG                              FG

ABV                             IBU

VOLUME                          EFFICIENCY

| $Ca^{+2}$ | $Mg^{+2}$ | $Na^+$ | $Cl^-$ | $So_4^{-2}$ | Alk | pH |
|---|---|---|---|---|---|---|
| | | | | | | |
| | | | | | | |

# 🌾 GRAIN

| | % | WEIGHT | GU |
|---|---|---|---|
| | | | |
| | | | |
| | | | |
| | | | |
| | | | |
| | | | |
| | | | |
| | | | |

# 💧 WATER

| | | | | |
|---|---|---|---|---|
| | | | | |
| | | | | |
| | | | | |

# 🕐 MASH

| | VOLUME | STRIKE° | REST° | TIME | GRAVITY |
|---|---|---|---|---|---|
| | | | | | |
| | | | | | |
| | | | | | |
| | | | | | |
| | | | | | |

15

# 🌾 HOPS

| | OZ | AA% | IBU | MIN |
|---|---|---|---|---|
| | | | | |
| | | | | |
| | | | | |
| | | | | |
| | | | | |
| | | | | |
| | | | | |
| | | | | |

# 🧪 YEAST

| | AMOUNT | PITCH° |
|---|---|---|
| | | |
| | | |

15

# 🕐 FERMENT

| | TIME | TEMP° | GRAVITY |
|---|---|---|---|
| | | | |
| | | | |
| | | | |
| | | | |
| | | | |

# 🍾 PACKAGE

| VOLUME | TEMP | CO2 | PRIME |
|--------|------|-----|-------|
|        |      |     |       |

# 🍺 NOTES

AROMA

APPEARANCE

FLAVOR

15

MOUTHFEEL

OVERALL

# BREW SIXTEEN

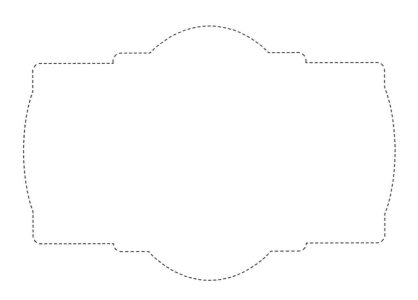

STYLE

BREWED

FINISHED

OG

FG

ABV

IBU

VOLUME

EFFICIENCY

| Ca$^{+2}$ | Mg$^{+2}$ | Na$^+$ | Cl$^-$ | So$_4$$^{-2}$ | Alk | pH |
|---|---|---|---|---|---|---|

## 🌾 GRAIN

| | % | WEIGHT | GU |
|---|---|---|---|
| | | | |
| | | | |
| | | | |
| | | | |
| | | | |
| | | | |
| | | | |
| | | | |
| | | | |

## 💧 WATER

| | | | |
|---|---|---|---|
| | | | |
| | | | |
| | | | |

## 🕐 MASH

| | VOLUME | STRIKE° | REST° | TIME | GRAVITY |
|---|---|---|---|---|---|
| | | | | | |
| | | | | | |
| | | | | | |
| | | | | | |
| | | | | | |

# 🌿 HOPS

| | OZ | AA% | IBU | MIN |
|---|---|---|---|---|
| | | | | |
| | | | | |
| | | | | |
| | | | | |
| | | | | |
| | | | | |
| | | | | |

# 🧪 YEAST

| | AMOUNT | PITCH° |
|---|---|---|
| | | |
| | | |

16

# 🕐 FERMENT

| | TIME | TEMP° | GRAVITY |
|---|---|---|---|
| | | | |
| | | | |
| | | | |
| | | | |

# 🍾 PACKAGE

| VOLUME | TEMP | CO2 | PRIME |
|--------|------|-----|-------|
|        |      |     |       |

# 🍺 NOTES

AROMA

APPEARANCE

FLAVOR

MOUTHFEEL

16

OVERALL

# BREW SEVENTEEN

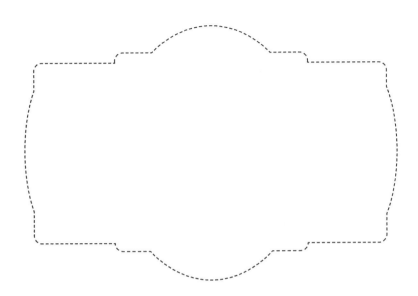

STYLE

BREWED                                        FINISHED

OG                                            FG

ABV                                           IBU

VOLUME                                        EFFICIENCY

$Ca^{+2}$        $Mg^{+2}$        $Na^+$        $Cl^-$        $So_4^{-2}$        Alk        pH

# 🌾 GRAIN

| | % | WEIGHT | GU |
|---|---|---|---|
| | | | |
| | | | |
| | | | |
| | | | |
| | | | |
| | | | |
| | | | |
| | | | |

# 💧 WATER

| | | | | |
|---|---|---|---|---|
| | | | | |
| | | | | |
| | | | | |

# 🕐 MASH

| | VOLUME | STRIKE° | REST° | TIME | GRAVITY |
|---|---|---|---|---|---|
| | | | | | |
| | | | | | |
| | | | | | |
| | | | | | |

# 🌿 HOPS

| | OZ | AA% | IBU | MIN |
|---|---|---|---|---|
| | | | | |
| | | | | |
| | | | | |
| | | | | |
| | | | | |
| | | | | |
| | | | | |

# 🧪 YEAST

| | AMOUNT | PITCH° |
|---|---|---|
| | | |

# 🕐 FERMENT

| | TIME | TEMP° | GRAVITY |
|---|---|---|---|
| | | | |
| | | | |
| | | | |
| | | | |

# 🍾 PACKAGE

| VOLUME | TEMP | CO2 | PRIME |
|--------|------|-----|-------|
|        |      |     |       |

# 🍺 NOTES

AROMA

APPEARANCE

FLAVOR

MOUTHFEEL

17

OVERALL

# BREW EIGHTEEN

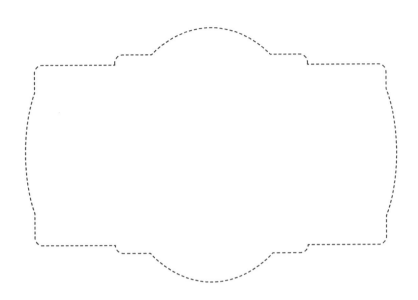

STYLE

BREWED                                    FINISHED

OG                                        FG

ABV                                       IBU

VOLUME                                    EFFICIENCY

$Ca^{+2}$      $Mg^{+2}$      $Na^+$      $Cl^-$      $So_4^{-2}$      Alk      pH

73

# 🌾 GRAIN

| | % | WEIGHT | GU |
|---|---|---|---|
| | | | |
| | | | |
| | | | |
| | | | |
| | | | |
| | | | |
| | | | |

# 💧 WATER

| | | | |
|---|---|---|---|
| | | | |
| | | | |

# 🕐 MASH

| | VOLUME | STRIKE° | REST° | TIME | GRAVITY |
|---|---|---|---|---|---|
| | | | | | |
| | | | | | |
| | | | | | |
| | | | | | |
| | | | | | |

18

# 🌿 HOPS

| | OZ | AA% | IBU | MIN |
|---|---|---|---|---|
| | | | | |
| | | | | |
| | | | | |
| | | | | |
| | | | | |
| | | | | |

# 🧪 YEAST

| | AMOUNT | PITCH° |
|---|---|---|
| | | |

# 🕐 FERMENT

| | TIME | TEMP° | GRAVITY |
|---|---|---|---|
| | | | |
| | | | |
| | | | |
| | | | |

18

# 🍾 PACKAGE

| | VOLUME | TEMP | CO2 | PRIME |
|---|---|---|---|---|
| | | | | |

# 🍺 NOTES

**AROMA**

**APPEARANCE**

**FLAVOR**

**MOUTHFEEL**

18

**OVERALL**

# INVENTORY

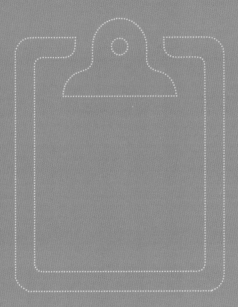

# HOPS

| NAME | AA% |
|------|-----|
| DATE | OZ |
| | |
| | |
| | |
| | |
| | |
| | |

| NAME | AA% |
|------|-----|
| DATE | OZ |
| | |
| | |
| | |
| | |
| | |
| | |

| NAME | AA% |
|------|-----|
| DATE | OZ |
| | |
| | |
| | |
| | |
| | |
| | |

| NAME | AA% |
|------|-----|
| DATE | OZ |
| | |
| | |
| | |
| | |
| | |
| | |

| NAME | AA% |
|------|-----|
| DATE | OZ |
| | |
| | |
| | |
| | |
| | |
| | |

| NAME | AA% |
|------|-----|
| DATE | OZ |
| | |
| | |
| | |
| | |
| | |
| | |

# HOPS

| NAME | AA% |
|------|-----|
| DATE | OZ |

| NAME | AA% |
|------|-----|
| DATE | OZ |

| NAME | AA% |
|------|-----|
| DATE | OZ |

| NAME | AA% |
|------|-----|
| DATE | OZ |

| NAME | AA% |
|------|-----|
| DATE | OZ |

| NAME | AA% |
|------|-----|
| DATE | OZ |

# GRAIN

| | NAME |
|---|---|
| **DATE** | **WEIGHT** |
| | |
| | |
| | |
| | |
| | |
| | |

| | NAME |
|---|---|
| **DATE** | **WEIGHT** |
| | |
| | |
| | |
| | |
| | |
| | |

| | NAME |
|---|---|
| **DATE** | **WEIGHT** |
| | |
| | |
| | |
| | |
| | |
| | |

| | NAME |
|---|---|
| **DATE** | **WEIGHT** |
| | |
| | |
| | |
| | |
| | |
| | |

| | NAME |
|---|---|
| **DATE** | **WEIGHT** |
| | |
| | |
| | |
| | |
| | |
| | |

| | NAME |
|---|---|
| **DATE** | **WEIGHT** |
| | |
| | |
| | |
| | |
| | |
| | |

# GRAIN

| | NAME |
|---|---|
| DATE | WEIGHT |
| | |
| | |
| | |
| | |
| | |
| | |

| | NAME |
|---|---|
| DATE | WEIGHT |
| | |
| | |
| | |
| | |
| | |
| | |

| | NAME |
|---|---|
| DATE | WEIGHT |
| | |
| | |
| | |
| | |
| | |
| | |

| | NAME |
|---|---|
| DATE | WEIGHT |
| | |
| | |
| | |
| | |
| | |
| | |

| | NAME |
|---|---|
| DATE | WEIGHT |
| | |
| | |
| | |
| | |
| | |
| | |

| | NAME |
|---|---|
| DATE | WEIGHT |
| | |
| | |
| | |
| | |
| | |
| | |

| MONTH | | | |
|---|---|---|---|
| SUNDAY | MONDAY | TUESDAY | WEDNESDAY |
| | | | |
| | | | |
| | | | |
| | | | |
| | | | |

| THURSDAY | FRIDAY | SATURDAY |
| --- | --- | --- |
|  |  |  |
|  |  |  |
|  |  |  |
|  |  |  |
|  |  |  |

MONTH

| SUNDAY | MONDAY | TUESDAY | WEDNESDAY |
|--------|--------|---------|-----------|
|        |        |         |           |
|        |        |         |           |
|        |        |         |           |
|        |        |         |           |
|        |        |         |           |

| THURSDAY | FRIDAY | SATURDAY |
|---|---|---|
|  |  |  |
|  |  |  |
|  |  |  |
|  |  |  |
|  |  |  |

| MONTH | | | |
|---|---|---|---|
| SUNDAY | MONDAY | TUESDAY | WEDNESDAY |
| | | | |
| | | | |
| | | | |
| | | | |
| | | | |

| THURSDAY | FRIDAY | SATURDAY |
|----------|--------|----------|
|          |        |          |
|          |        |          |
|          |        |          |
|          |        |          |
|          |        |          |

MONTH

| SUNDAY | MONDAY | TUESDAY | WEDNESDAY |
|--------|--------|---------|-----------|
|        |        |         |           |
|        |        |         |           |
|        |        |         |           |
|        |        |         |           |
|        |        |         |           |

| THURSDAY | FRIDAY | SATURDAY |
| --- | --- | --- |
| | | |
| | | |
| | | |
| | | |
| | | |

MONTH

| SUNDAY | MONDAY | TUESDAY | WEDNESDAY |
|--------|--------|---------|-----------|
|        |        |         |           |
|        |        |         |           |
|        |        |         |           |
|        |        |         |           |
|        |        |         |           |

| THURSDAY | FRIDAY | SATURDAY |
| --- | --- | --- |
|  |  |  |
|  |  |  |
|  |  |  |
|  |  |  |
|  |  |  |

MONTH

| SUNDAY | MONDAY | TUESDAY | WEDNESDAY |
| --- | --- | --- | --- |
| | | | |
| | | | |
| | | | |
| | | | |
| | | | |

| THURSDAY | FRIDAY | SATURDAY |
|----------|--------|----------|
|          |        |          |
|          |        |          |
|          |        |          |
|          |        |          |
|          |        |          |

# REFERENCE

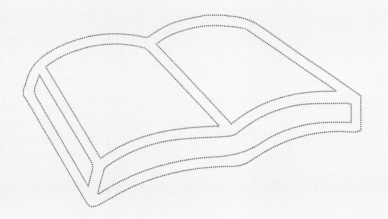

$f_{(x)}$

## ABV%

ABV% = (ORIGINAL GRAVITY - FINAL GRAVITY) * 131

## ALPHA ACID UNITS

AAU = WEIGHT (OZ) X % ALPHA ACIDS (WHOLE NUMBER)

## APPARENT ATTENUATION

$$AA\% = \frac{(ORIGINAL\ GRAVITY - FINAL\ GRAVITY)}{(ORIGINAL\ GRAVITY - 1)\ X\ 100} \times 100$$

## EXTRACT POTENTIAL OF FERMENTABLES

| MASH INGREDIENTS | EXTRACT POTENTIAL (1 LB. IN 1 GAL.) |
| --- | --- |
| CHOCOLATE | 1.033 - 1.035 (DARKER = LOWER EXTRACT) |
| BLACK | 1.025 |
| ROAST | 1.025 - 1.030 |
| CHRYSTAL / CARA | 1.033 - 1.035 |
| MUNICH / VIENNA / MILD / BISCUIT | 1.035 - 1.036 |
| PALE / PILSNER | 1.035 - 1.037 |
| CORN | 1.037 - 1.039 |
| OATS | 1.033 |
| RYE | 1.029 |
| WHEAT (MALTED) | 1.037 - 1.040 |
| WHEAT / RYE (UNMALTED OR FLAKED) | 1.036 |

### BOIL KETTLE FERMENTABLES*

| | |
| --- | --- |
| CANE SUGAR | 1.046 |
| CORN SUGAR | 1.037 |
| DRY EXTRACT | 1.045 |
| HONEY | 1.035 |
| LIQUID EXTRACT | 1.037 - 1.039 |
| MAPLE SYRUP | 1.030 |
| MOLASSES | 1.036 |

*ADD DIRECTLY TO KETTLE, EFFICIENCY FACTOR = 1.00

# FORCE CARBONATION CHART

TEMPERATURE × PSI

| °F | 1 | 2 | 3 | 4 | 5 | 6 | 7 | 8 | 9 | 10 | 11 | 12 | 13 | 14 | 15 | 16 | 17 | 18 | 19 | 20 | 21 | 22 | 23 | 24 | 25 | 26 | 27 | 28 | 29 | 30 |
|---|---|---|---|---|---|---|---|---|---|---|---|---|---|---|---|---|---|---|---|---|---|---|---|---|---|---|---|---|---|---|
| 30°F | 1.82 | 1.92 | 2.03 | 2.14 | 2.23 | 2.36 | 2.48 | 2.60 | 2.70 | 2.82 | 2.93 | 3.02 | 3.13 | 3.24 | 3.35 | 3.46 | 3.57 | 3.67 | 3.78 | 3.89 | 4.00 | 4.11 | 4.22 | 4.33 | 4.44 | 4.55 | 4.66 | 4.77 | 4.87 | 4.98 |
| 31°F | 1.78 | 1.88 | 2.00 | 2.10 | 2.20 | 2.31 | 2.42 | 2.54 | 2.65 | 2.76 | 2.86 | 2.96 | 3.07 | 3.17 | 3.28 | 3.39 | 3.50 | 3.60 | 3.71 | 3.82 | 3.93 | 4.03 | 4.14 | 4.25 | 4.35 | 4.46 | 4.57 | 4.68 | 4.78 | 4.89 |
| 32°F | 1.75 | 1.85 | 1.95 | 2.05 | 2.15 | 2.27 | 2.38 | 2.48 | 2.59 | 2.70 | 2.80 | 2.90 | 3.00 | 3.11 | 3.21 | 3.31 | 3.42 | 3.52 | 3.63 | 3.73 | 3.84 | 3.94 | 4.04 | 4.15 | 4.25 | 4.36 | 4.46 | 4.57 | 4.67 | 4.77 |
| 33°F | 1.71 | 1.81 | 1.91 | 2.01 | 2.10 | 2.23 | 2.33 | 2.43 | 2.53 | 2.63 | 2.74 | 2.84 | 2.96 | 3.06 | 3.15 | 3.25 | 3.35 | 3.46 | 3.56 | 3.66 | 3.76 | 3.87 | 3.97 | 4.07 | 4.18 | 4.28 | 4.38 | 4.48 | 4.59 | 4.69 |
| 34°F | 1.68 | 1.78 | 1.86 | 1.97 | 2.06 | 2.18 | 2.28 | 2.38 | 2.48 | 2.58 | 2.69 | 2.79 | 2.90 | 3.00 | 3.09 | 3.19 | 3.29 | 3.39 | 3.49 | 3.59 | 3.69 | 3.79 | 3.90 | 4.00 | 4.10 | 4.20 | 4.30 | 4.40 | 4.50 | 4.60 |
| 35°F | 1.63 | 1.73 | 1.83 | 1.93 | 2.02 | 2.14 | 2.24 | 2.34 | 2.43 | 2.52 | 2.63 | 2.73 | 2.83 | 2.93 | 3.02 | 3.12 | 3.22 | 3.32 | 3.42 | 3.52 | 3.62 | 3.72 | 3.82 | 3.92 | 4.01 | 4.11 | 4.21 | 4.31 | 4.41 | 4.51 |
| 36°F | 1.60 | 1.69 | 1.79 | 1.88 | 1.98 | 2.09 | 2.19 | 2.29 | 2.38 | 2.47 | 2.57 | 2.67 | 2.77 | 2.86 | 2.96 | 3.05 | 3.15 | 3.24 | 3.34 | 3.43 | 3.53 | 3.63 | 3.72 | 3.82 | 3.92 | 4.01 | 4.11 | 4.21 | 4.30 | 4.40 |
| 37°F | 1.55 | 1.65 | 1.74 | 1.84 | 1.94 | 2.04 | 2.14 | 2.24 | 2.33 | 2.42 | 2.52 | 2.62 | 2.71 | 2.80 | 2.90 | 3.00 | 3.09 | 3.18 | 3.27 | 3.37 | 3.46 | 3.56 | 3.65 | 3.75 | 3.84 | 3.94 | 4.03 | 4.13 | 4.22 | 4.32 |
| 38°F | 1.52 | 1.61 | 1.71 | 1.80 | 1.90 | 2.00 | 2.10 | 2.19 | 2.29 | 2.38 | 2.48 | 2.57 | 2.66 | 2.75 | 2.85 | 2.94 | 3.03 | 3.12 | 3.21 | 3.30 | 3.40 | 3.49 | 3.59 | 3.68 | 3.77 | 3.87 | 3.96 | 4.06 | 4.15 | 4.24 |
| 39°F | 1.49 | 1.58 | 1.67 | 1.77 | 1.86 | 1.96 | 2.06 | 2.15 | 2.25 | 2.34 | 2.43 | 2.52 | 2.61 | 2.70 | 2.80 | 2.89 | 2.98 | 3.07 | 3.16 | 3.25 | 3.34 | 3.44 | 3.53 | 3.62 | 3.71 | 3.81 | 3.90 | 3.99 | 4.08 | 4.18 |
| 40°F | 1.47 | 1.56 | 1.65 | 1.74 | 1.83 | 1.92 | 2.01 | 2.10 | 2.20 | 2.30 | 2.39 | 2.47 | 2.56 | 2.65 | 2.75 | 2.84 | 2.93 | 3.01 | 3.10 | 3.19 | 3.28 | 3.37 | 3.46 | 3.55 | 3.64 | 3.73 | 3.82 | 3.91 | 4.01 | 4.10 |
| 41°F | 1.43 | 1.52 | 1.61 | 1.70 | 1.79 | 1.88 | 1.97 | 2.06 | 2.16 | 2.25 | 2.34 | 2.43 | 2.52 | 2.60 | 2.70 | 2.79 | 2.88 | 2.96 | 3.05 | 3.14 | 3.23 | 3.32 | 3.41 | 3.50 | 3.59 | 3.68 | 3.77 | 3.86 | 3.95 | 4.04 |
| 42°F | 1.39 | 1.48 | 1.57 | 1.66 | 1.75 | 1.85 | 1.94 | 2.02 | 2.12 | 2.21 | 2.30 | 2.39 | 2.48 | 2.56 | 2.65 | 2.74 | 2.83 | 2.91 | 3.00 | 3.09 | 3.18 | 3.26 | 3.35 | 3.44 | 3.53 | 3.62 | 3.70 | 3.79 | 3.88 | 3.97 |
| 43°F | 1.37 | 1.46 | 1.54 | 1.63 | 1.72 | 1.81 | 1.90 | 1.99 | 2.08 | 2.17 | 2.26 | 2.35 | 2.43 | 2.52 | 2.61 | 2.70 | 2.78 | 2.86 | 2.95 | 3.04 | 3.13 | 3.21 | 3.30 | 3.39 | 3.47 | 3.56 | 3.65 | 3.74 | 3.82 | 3.91 |
| 44°F | 1.35 | 1.43 | 1.52 | 1.60 | 1.69 | 1.78 | 1.87 | 1.95 | 2.04 | 2.13 | 2.22 | 2.30 | 2.39 | 2.47 | 2.56 | 2.64 | 2.73 | 2.81 | 2.90 | 2.99 | 3.07 | 3.16 | 3.24 | 3.33 | 3.41 | 3.50 | 3.58 | 3.67 | 3.76 | 3.84 |
| 45°F | 1.32 | 1.41 | 1.49 | 1.58 | 1.66 | 1.75 | 1.84 | 1.91 | 2.00 | 2.08 | 2.17 | 2.26 | 2.34 | 2.42 | 2.51 | 2.60 | 2.69 | 2.77 | 2.86 | 2.94 | 3.02 | 3.11 | 3.19 | 3.28 | 3.36 | 3.45 | 3.53 | 3.62 | 3.70 | 3.79 |
| 46°F | 1.28 | 1.37 | 1.45 | 1.54 | 1.62 | 1.71 | 1.80 | 1.88 | 1.96 | 2.04 | 2.13 | 2.22 | 2.30 | 2.38 | 2.47 | 2.55 | 2.64 | 2.72 | 2.81 | 2.89 | 2.98 | 3.06 | 3.15 | 3.23 | 3.31 | 3.40 | 3.48 | 3.57 | 3.65 | 3.74 |
| 47°F | 1.26 | 1.34 | 1.42 | 1.51 | 1.59 | 1.68 | 1.76 | 1.84 | 1.92 | 2.00 | 2.09 | 2.18 | 2.26 | 2.34 | 2.42 | 2.50 | 2.59 | 2.67 | 2.76 | 2.84 | 2.93 | 3.02 | 3.09 | 3.18 | 3.26 | 3.35 | 3.43 | 3.51 | 3.60 | 3.68 |
| 48°F | 1.23 | 1.31 | 1.39 | 1.48 | 1.56 | 1.65 | 1.73 | 1.81 | 1.89 | 1.96 | 2.05 | 2.14 | 2.22 | 2.30 | 2.38 | 2.46 | 2.54 | 2.62 | 2.71 | 2.79 | 2.88 | 2.96 | 3.04 | 3.13 | 3.21 | 3.30 | 3.38 | 3.46 | 3.54 | 3.63 |
| 49°F | 1.21 | 1.29 | 1.37 | 1.45 | 1.53 | 1.62 | 1.70 | 1.79 | 1.86 | 1.93 | 2.01 | 2.10 | 2.18 | 2.25 | 2.34 | 2.42 | 2.50 | 2.58 | 2.67 | 2.75 | 2.83 | 2.91 | 3.00 | 3.07 | 3.15 | 3.23 | 3.31 | 3.39 | 3.47 | 3.56 |
| 50°F | 1.18 | 1.26 | 1.34 | 1.42 | 1.50 | 1.59 | 1.66 | 1.74 | 1.82 | 1.90 | 1.98 | 2.06 | 2.14 | 2.21 | 2.30 | 2.38 | 2.46 | 2.54 | 2.62 | 2.70 | 2.78 | 2.86 | 2.94 | 3.02 | 3.10 | 3.17 | 3.25 | 3.33 | 3.41 | 3.49 |
| 51°F | 1.18 | 1.26 | 1.34 | 1.42 | 1.49 | 1.57 | 1.64 | 1.71 | 1.79 | 1.87 | 1.95 | 2.02 | 2.10 | 2.18 | 2.26 | 2.34 | 2.42 | 2.49 | 2.57 | 2.65 | 2.74 | 2.82 | 2.90 | 2.97 | 3.05 | 3.13 | 3.19 | 3.27 | 3.34 | 3.42 |
| 52°F | 1.16 | 1.23 | 1.31 | 1.39 | 1.46 | 1.54 | 1.61 | 1.68 | 1.76 | 1.84 | 1.92 | 1.99 | 2.06 | 2.14 | 2.22 | 2.30 | 2.38 | 2.45 | 2.53 | 2.61 | 2.68 | 2.76 | 2.84 | 2.92 | 3.00 | 3.06 | 3.13 | 3.22 | 3.30 | 3.37 |
| 53°F | 1.14 | 1.21 | 1.29 | 1.36 | 1.43 | 1.51 | 1.59 | 1.66 | 1.73 | 1.81 | 1.89 | 1.96 | 2.03 | 2.10 | 2.18 | 2.26 | 2.34 | 2.41 | 2.49 | 2.57 | 2.64 | 2.71 | 2.79 | 2.86 | 2.94 | 3.01 | 3.09 | 3.16 | 3.24 | 3.31 |
| 54°F | 1.12 | 1.19 | 1.27 | 1.34 | 1.41 | 1.49 | 1.56 | 1.63 | 1.71 | 1.78 | 1.86 | 1.93 | 2.00 | 2.07 | 2.15 | 2.22 | 2.30 | 2.37 | 2.45 | 2.52 | 2.59 | 2.66 | 2.74 | 2.81 | 2.89 | 2.96 | 3.04 | 3.10 | 3.17 | 3.24 |
| 55°F | 1.10 | 1.17 | 1.24 | 1.31 | 1.39 | 1.46 | 1.53 | 1.60 | 1.68 | 1.75 | 1.82 | 1.89 | 1.97 | 2.04 | 2.12 | 2.18 | 2.26 | 2.33 | 2.40 | 2.47 | 2.54 | 2.62 | 2.69 | 2.76 | 2.83 | 2.89 | 2.97 | 3.04 | 3.11 | 3.18 |
| 56°F | 1.07 | 1.15 | 1.22 | 1.29 | 1.36 | 1.43 | 1.50 | 1.57 | 1.65 | 1.72 | 1.79 | 1.86 | 1.93 | 2.00 | 2.08 | 2.15 | 2.22 | 2.29 | 2.36 | 2.43 | 2.50 | 2.57 | 2.64 | 2.71 | 2.78 | 2.85 | 2.92 | 2.99 | 3.06 | 3.13 |
| 57°F | 1.05 | 1.12 | 1.19 | 1.26 | 1.33 | 1.40 | 1.47 | 1.54 | 1.62 | 1.70 | 1.77 | 1.83 | 1.90 | 1.97 | 2.04 | 2.11 | 2.18 | 2.25 | 2.32 | 2.39 | 2.46 | 2.53 | 2.59 | 2.66 | 2.73 | 2.80 | 2.87 | 2.94 | 3.00 | 3.08 |
| 58°F | 1.03 | 1.10 | 1.17 | 1.24 | 1.31 | 1.37 | 1.44 | 1.51 | 1.59 | 1.67 | 1.74 | 1.80 | 1.87 | 1.94 | 2.01 | 2.08 | 2.15 | 2.21 | 2.28 | 2.35 | 2.42 | 2.48 | 2.55 | 2.62 | 2.69 | 2.75 | 2.82 | 2.88 | 2.95 | 3.02 |
| 59°F | 1.02 | 1.09 | 1.16 | 1.22 | 1.29 | 1.36 | 1.42 | 1.49 | 1.56 | 1.64 | 1.71 | 1.77 | 1.84 | 1.91 | 1.98 | 2.04 | 2.11 | 2.17 | 2.24 | 2.31 | 2.38 | 2.43 | 2.50 | 2.57 | 2.64 | 2.70 | 2.77 | 2.84 | 2.91 | 2.97 |
| 60°F | 1.01 | 1.08 | 1.15 | 1.21 | 1.28 | 1.34 | 1.41 | 1.47 | 1.54 | 1.62 | 1.69 | 1.75 | 1.82 | 1.88 | 1.95 | 2.01 | 2.08 | 2.14 | 2.21 | 2.27 | 2.34 | 2.40 | 2.47 | 2.53 | 2.60 | 2.66 | 2.73 | 2.79 | 2.86 | 2.92 |
| 61°F | 0.99 | 1.05 | 1.12 | 1.18 | 1.24 | 1.31 | 1.37 | 1.44 | 1.50 | 1.57 | 1.63 | 1.69 | 1.76 | 1.82 | 1.89 | 1.95 | 2.02 | 2.08 | 2.14 | 2.21 | 2.27 | 2.34 | 2.40 | 2.47 | 2.53 | 2.59 | 2.66 | 2.72 | 2.79 | 2.85 |
| 62°F | 0.96 | 1.02 | 1.09 | 1.15 | 1.21 | 1.27 | 1.34 | 1.40 | 1.46 | 1.52 | 1.59 | 1.65 | 1.71 | 1.78 | 1.84 | 1.90 | 1.97 | 2.03 | 2.09 | 2.15 | 2.22 | 2.28 | 2.34 | 2.41 | 2.47 | 2.53 | 2.59 | 2.66 | 2.72 | 2.78 |
| 63°F | 0.93 | 0.99 | 1.06 | 1.12 | 1.18 | 1.24 | 1.30 | 1.36 | 1.42 | 1.49 | 1.55 | 1.61 | 1.67 | 1.73 | 1.79 | 1.85 | 1.92 | 1.98 | 2.04 | 2.10 | 2.16 | 2.22 | 2.28 | 2.35 | 2.41 | 2.47 | 2.53 | 2.59 | 2.65 | 2.71 |
| 64°F | 0.91 | 0.97 | 1.03 | 1.09 | 1.15 | 1.21 | 1.27 | 1.33 | 1.39 | 1.45 | 1.51 | 1.57 | 1.63 | 1.69 | 1.75 | 1.81 | 1.87 | 1.93 | 1.99 | 2.05 | 2.11 | 2.17 | 2.23 | 2.29 | 2.35 | 2.41 | 2.47 | 2.52 | 2.58 | 2.64 |
| 65°F | 0.88 | 0.94 | 1.00 | 1.06 | 1.11 | 1.17 | 1.23 | 1.29 | 1.35 | 1.41 | 1.46 | 1.52 | 1.58 | 1.64 | 1.70 | 1.76 | 1.82 | 1.87 | 1.93 | 1.99 | 2.05 | 2.11 | 2.17 | 2.23 | 2.28 | 2.34 | 2.40 | 2.46 | 2.52 | 2.58 |

$f(x)$

## GRAVITY CORRECTION FOR TEMPERATURE

| TEMP °F (°C) | ADD SG |
|---|---|
| 80 (27) | 0.002 |
| 90 (32) | 0.004 |
| 100 (38) | 0.006 |
| 110 (43) | 0.008 |
| 120 (49) | 0.010 |
| 130 (54) | 0.013 |
| 140 (60) | 0.016 |
| 150 (66) | 0.018 |
| 160 (71) | 0.022 |
| 170 (77) | 0.025 |
| 190 (88) | 0.033 |
| 212 (100) | 0.040 |

## GRAVITY UNITS

GU = (SPECIFIC GRAVITY - 1) x 1,000

Shorthand 1.053 = 53 GU

## INGREDIENT GRAVITY UNITS

IGU = INGREDIENT % of TOTAL GRIST x TOTAL GRAVITY UNITS

## INITIAL INFUSION

STRIKE WATER TEMPERATURE = $(.2/R)(T_S - T_G) + T_S$

$T_S$ = Target temperature (°F) of the mash

$T_G$ = Initial temperature (°F) of the grain

R = Ratio of water to grain (quarts per pound)

## INTERNATIONAL BITTERNESS UNITS

$$IBU = \frac{AAU \times UTILIZATION \times 75}{RECIPE\ VOLUME}$$

## HOP UTILIZATION
### TIME X GRAVITY

|     | 1.030 | 1.040 | 1.050 | 1.060 | 1.070 | 1.080 | 1.090 | 1.100 | 1.110 | 1.120 |
|-----|-------|-------|-------|-------|-------|-------|-------|-------|-------|-------|
| 0   | 0.000 | 0.000 | 0.000 | 0.000 | 0.000 | 0.000 | 0.000 | 0.000 | 0.000 | 0.000 |
| 5   | 0.055 | 0.050 | 0.046 | 0.042 | 0.038 | 0.035 | 0.032 | 0.029 | 0.027 | 0.025 |
| 10  | 0.100 | 0.091 | 0.084 | 0.076 | 0.070 | 0.064 | 0.058 | 0.053 | 0.049 | 0.045 |
| 15  | 0.137 | 0.125 | 0.114 | 0.105 | 0.096 | 0.087 | 0.080 | 0.073 | 0.067 | 0.061 |
| 20  | 0.167 | 0.153 | 0.140 | 0.128 | 0.117 | 0.107 | 0.098 | 0.089 | 0.081 | 0.074 |
| 25  | 0.192 | 0.175 | 0.160 | 0.147 | 0.134 | 0.122 | 0.112 | 0.102 | 0.094 | 0.085 |
| 30  | 0.212 | 0.194 | 0.177 | 0.162 | 0.148 | 0.135 | 0.124 | 0.113 | 0.103 | 0.094 |
| 35  | 0.229 | 0.209 | 0.191 | 0.175 | 0.160 | 0.146 | 0.133 | 0.122 | 0.111 | 0.102 |
| 40  | 0.242 | 0.221 | 0.202 | 0.185 | 0.169 | 0.155 | 0.141 | 0.129 | 0.118 | 0.108 |
| 45  | 0.253 | 0.232 | 0.212 | 0.194 | 0.177 | 0.162 | 0.148 | 0.135 | 0.123 | 0.113 |
| 50  | 0.263 | 0.240 | 0.219 | 0.200 | 0.183 | 0.168 | 0.153 | 0.140 | 0.128 | 0.117 |
| 55  | 0.270 | 0.247 | 0.226 | 0.206 | 0.188 | 0.172 | 0.157 | 0.144 | 0.132 | 0.120 |
| 60  | 0.276 | 0.252 | 0.231 | 0.211 | 0.193 | 0.176 | 0.161 | 0.147 | 0.135 | 0.123 |
| 70  | 0.285 | 0.261 | 0.238 | 0.218 | 0.199 | 0.182 | 0.166 | 0.152 | 0.139 | 0.127 |
| 80  | 0.291 | 0.266 | 0.243 | 0.222 | 0.203 | 0.186 | 0.170 | 0.155 | 0.142 | 0.130 |
| 90  | 0.295 | 0.270 | 0.247 | 0.226 | 0.206 | 0.188 | 0.172 | 0.157 | 0.144 | 0.132 |
| 100 | 0.298 | 0.272 | 0.249 | 0.228 | 0.208 | 0.190 | 0.174 | 0.159 | 0.145 | 0.133 |
| 110 | 0.300 | 0.274 | 0.251 | 0.229 | 0.209 | 0.191 | 0.175 | 0.160 | 0.146 | 0.134 |
| 120 | 0.301 | 0.275 | 0.252 | 0.230 | 0.210 | 0.192 | 0.176 | 0.161 | 0.147 | 0.134 |

## MALT GRAVITY PER POUND

$G_{LB}$ = (TOTAL EXTRACT POTENTIAL) X MASH EFFICIENCY

## MALT POUNDS NEEDED

$$M_{1b} = \frac{\text{INGREDIENT GRAVITY UNITS}}{\text{GRAVITY PER LB OF MALT}}$$

## MASH EFFICIENCY

$$\text{EFICIENCY} = \frac{\text{Total Gravity of Wort}}{\text{Total Potential Gravity of Grains}}$$

## MASH INFUSION

$$\text{INFUSION WATER QUARTS NEEDED} = \frac{(T_T - T_M)(.2G + W_M)}{(T_W - T_T)}$$

$T_T$ = Target temperature (°F) of the mash

$T_M$ = Initial temperature (oF) of the mash

$G$ = Amount of grain in the mash (pounds)

$W_M$ = Total amount of water in the mash (quarts)

$T_W$ = Actual temperature (°F) of the infusion water

## TOTAL GRAVITY UNITS PER BATCH

TGU = GRAVITY UNITS X BATCH VOLUME IN GALLONS

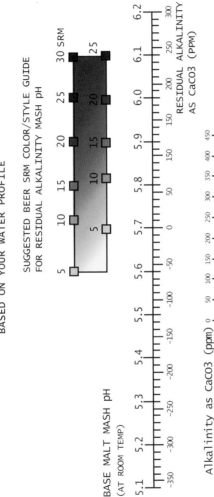

## APPROXIMATE pH OF 100% BASE MALT MASH
### BASED ON YOUR WATER PROFILE

SUGGESTED BEER SRM COLOR/STYLE GUIDE
FOR RESIDUAL ALKALINITY MASH pH

BASE MALT MASH pH
(AT ROOM TEMP)

RESIDUAL ALKALINITY
AS CaCO3 (PPM)

[HCO3] (ppm)

Effective Hardness

Alkalinity as CaCO3 (ppm)

[Mg] (ppm)

[Ca] (ppm)

## PRIMING SUGAR NOMOGRAPH
### FOR 5 US GALLONS

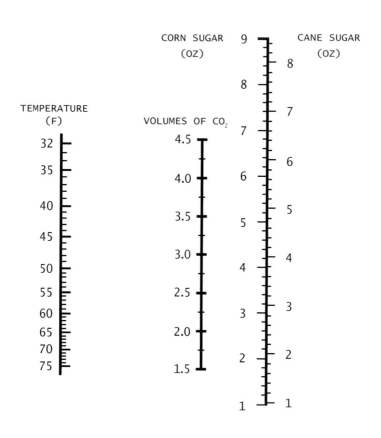

# USING BREWERS' LEDGER

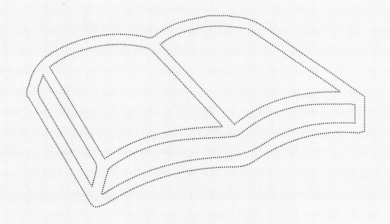

i

This book is for brewers of all levels who want to record every step while making beer. It follows the brewing process and provides fields that allow for consistent record keeping and quick comparison between batches. You'll find it handy, intuitive and useful, but it's also designed to be hacked so you can customize it easily to fit your record-keeping needs.

## BATCH

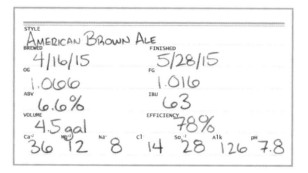

| NUMBER | The batch number corresponds with the table of contents. |
|---|---|
| LABEL | Great for doodline label art and naming your beer. |
| STYLE | Type of beer according to the BJCP style guide. |
| BREWED | Date you brew your beer. |
| FINISHED | Date you packaged your beer. |
| OG | Original Gravity. |
| FG | Final Gravity. |
| ABV | Alcohol by volume of finished beer. |
| IBU | Calculated bitterness of your beer. |
| VOLUME | Final packaged volume. |
| EFFICIENCY | Mash efficiency or total brewhouse efficiency. |
| WATER PROFILE | Your brewing water profile. |

# MALT

| 🌾 MALT | % | WEIGHT | GU |
|---|---|---|---|
| MARIS OTTER | 75 | 12# | 247.5 |
| WHEAT | 6.25 | 1# | 20.6 |
| CARA Pils | 7.8 | 1.25# | 25.7 |
| CRYSTAL 40° | 7.8 | 1.25# | 25.7 |
| CHOCOLATE 420° | 3.2 | .5# | 10.4 |
| | | 16# | 330 |

| | |
|---|---|
| MALT | List every grain and fermentable used. |
| % | Ingredient percent of grain bill. |
| WEIGHT | Measured amount of each ingredient. |
| GU | Ingredient Gravity Units<br><br>If GU isn't your thing, re-use this column for maltster, SRM, potential, or something else you'd like to record. |

# WATER

| 💧 WATER | CaCl | GYP | LACTIC | | VOL |
|---|---|---|---|---|---|
| MASH IN | 4.5g | 3.0g | 2ml | | 4.1 |
| SPARGE | 4.5g | 3.0g | -- | | 5.6 |

**Blank Fields** are for recording water treatments and additions for each step, as well as source and filterning notes

## MASH

| ⏱ MASH | VOLUME | STRIKE° | REST° | TIME | GRAVITY |
|---|---|---|---|---|---|
| MASH IN | 4.1 | 163° | 154°/152° | 60 | |
| SPARGE | 5.6 | 200° | 168° | 30 | |
| PRE BOIL | 7.5 | | | 10:15 | 1.056 |
| POST BOIL | 5.5 | | | 12:15 | 1.066 |
| FERMENTOR | 5.0 | | 67° | 12:45 | 1.066 |

| MASH | List every step, including pre- and post-boil, and wort into fermentor. |
|---|---|
| VOLUME | Amount of liquid for every step. |
| STRIKE° | Infusion temperature of each water addition. |
| REST° | Temperature of each step in your schedule. <br> (Tip: Draw a diagonal line through the box to record target versus actual temperature.) |
| TIME | The length of each step. <br> (Tip: Draw a diagonal line through the box to record length of time and time of day.) |
| GRAVITY | Record your gravity after each step to track efficiency. |

## HOPS

| 🌺 HOPS | OZ | AA% | IBU | MIN |
|---|---|---|---|---|
| NORTHERN BREWER | 2.0 | 6.5 | 49.2 | FWH/10:45 |
| NORTHERN BREWER | 1.0 | 6.5 | 7.1 | 15/11:15 |
| YEAST NUTRIENT | 1 tsp | | | 15 |
| IRISH MOSS | 1 cap | | | 15 |
| CASCADE (LEAF) | 2.0 | 6.0 | 6.8 | 5/12:10 |
| CENTENNIAL | 2.0 | 9.0 | | 5 DAY DRY |

| HOPS | Variety and type of each boil addition. (pellet, leaf, wet, etc) |
|---|---|
| OZ | The weight of each addition in ounces. |
| AA% | Alpha acids of each hop variety. |
| IBU | Calculated IBU for each addition. |
| MIN | Number of minutes each addition is boiled. <br> (Tip: Draw a diagonal line through the box to record minutes boiled and time of day) |

# YEAST

| 🧪 YEAST | | AMOUNT | PITCH° |
|---|---|---|---|
| WLP001 | | 1 VIAL | 67° |
| ○ 2 LITER STARTER, DECANTED | | | |
| ○ 60 SECONDS PURE $O_2$ | | | |

| YEAST | Strain and source. |
|---|---|
| | (Tip: Extend vertical lines to list multiple strains) |
| AMOUNT | How much yeast used in cell count or number of packages. |
| PITCH° | Temperature yeast is pitched. |

**Blank lines** for notes on propagation, aeration, nutrients, or others you feel necessary.

# FERMENT

| 🕐 FERMENT | DATE | TEMP° | GRAVITY |
|---|---|---|---|
| PRIMARY | 4/16 | 67 | 1.066 |
| REST | 4/20 | 71 | 1.018 |
| SECONDARY | 4/22 | 60 | 1.016 |
| FINISH | 5/28 | | 1.016 |

| FERMENT | Record primary, secondary and other steps of fermentation. |
|---|---|
| DATE | The date of each step. |
| TEMP | Temperature during each step |
| GRAVITY | Track gravity of each step during fermentation |

# PACKAGE

| 🍾 PACKAGE | VOLUME | TEMP | CO2 | PRIME |
|---|---|---|---|---|
| KEG 5/28/15 | 4.5gal | 38° | 2.5vol | 11psi |

| PACKAGE | Note the step and date on the left. |
|---|---|
| VOLUME | Final volume of your batch. |
| TEMP | Carbonation temperature when kegging or bottling. |
| $CO_2$ | Volumes of $CO_2$. |
| PRIME | Amount of priming sugar for bottling, or PSI when kegging. |

**Blank lines** allow for notes or steps in packaging.

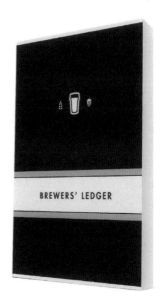